TRIUMPH
BOOKS
CHICAGO

Contributors

Photography
AP/Wide World Photo
David Durochik/SportPics
Tom DiPace

Linc Wonham ... Editor
Ray Ramos ... Designer

This book is available in quantity at special discounts for your group or organization. For further information, contact:

Triumph Books
601 South LaSalle Street
Suite 500
Chicago, Illinois 60605
(312) 939-3330
Fax (312) 663-3557

Printed in the United States of America

ISBN 1-57243-536-4

Like Mike

Ichiro Suzuki is a good, common Japanese name, comparable to your everyday John Smith in America. Ichiro means "first-born son." And Suzuki? Well, it's virtually every man's tagline in the land of the rising sun.

Several years ago when Akira Ogi stepped in as the manager of the Orix Blue Waves, one of his first moves was to replace the "Suzuki" on the back of his young star's uniform with "Ichiro."

"At first he was ashamed of that name," said Akiko Yamawaki, a journalist who covers baseball for *Jiji Press*, a Japanese newswire agency. After all, the Japanese find it extremely distasteful if a person seeks accolades beyond his status in any phase of society.

However, it quickly became clear that Ichiro's legions of fans loved the honor that had been bestowed upon their hero.

There have been scant few athletes worldwide to enjoy a truly first-name relationship with their adoring publics. Herman Ruth, it seems, was always the "Babe" to an America that loved him in the twenties and thirties. Another blast from the past was Pelé in soccer, whose athletic antics stirred passions among fans on just about every continent.

Perhaps the most overwhelming example, though, is a certain Michael of basketball fame. Mr. Jordan spent much of his young adulthood electrifying the entire planet with his leaping majesty.

No location seemed more caught up in this Jordan phenomenon than Japan. Magazines, newspapers, television, radio: virtually every Japanese media outlet tracked the exploits of "His Royal Airness" as he vanquished his many evil opponents—the Celtics and

Pistons and Lakers and Blazers and Sonics and Jazz—on his way to leading the Chicago Bulls to six National Basketball Association championships between 1991 and 1998.

With Jordan's legend growing so fast in Japan, it wasn't long before thousands of Japanese each year were saving their money to make pilgrimages to Chicago, Illinois, to worship at the Jordan shrine. A tour business quickly sprouted just to accommodate Michael's many Japanese fans. Tour-bus after tour-bus would take a spin past his suburban Chicago home and downtown restaurant, then on to the United Center for an opportunity to marvel at his statue there, and, hopefully, for a chance to see him play.

Among those thousands making the journey was Ichiro himself, a fan of Jordan's intense competitiveness and dedication to his sport. In fact, Ichiro went several times to observe this wonder known to his fans simply as "Mike," "Michael," or "MJ."

> **Then he would unleash his talent in a whirlwind of batting and fielding fury, carving up the best offerings of pitchers and chasing down balls in the outfield.**

Like Mike, Ichiro was amassing his own fame in Japan—not as some leaping wizard, but as a warrior all the same. Ichiro approached baseball like a samurai, those ancient Japanese warriors revered for their heart and discipline and skill with a sword. He would spend time before games meditating, or lost in deep concentration studying videotape of his opponent, or scouring the latest scouting reports. Then, at game time, he would unleash his talent in a whirlwind of batting and fielding fury, carving up the best offerings of opposing pitchers and chasing down balls in the outfield.

It's worth noting that Michael, too, has been something of a Zen warrior, having been directed in the art of meditation by his former coach, Phil Jackson. Working with psychologist George Mumford, Michael learned to use meditation and mindfulness to prepare for NBA games. During contests Jordan would go about his business with a mix of carefree ease and fierce determination, what he came to describe as "being in the moment," a state of total concentration. It's something Ichiro also seems to have mastered.

"The way he hits is just like a samurai," observed Isao Ogata, a 45-year-old office worker and baseball fan who frequents Tokyo's Jingu Stadium. "I'll bet he could split a mosquito with a sword."

He certainly showed that he could split the hopes of opponents. Ichiro launched his pro career shortly after MJ began his run of championships, and soon the speedy young outfielder with the rocket arm and the true bat began dominating the Japanese game. He won the league batting title seven straight years and hit for the highest percentage in the history of the eastern game, just the kind of performance to spur an outpouring of support.

Michael Jordan

That success made Ichiro a cultural icon in his homeland. "Ichiro is so big in Japan, Like Michael," Yamawaki, who also covers the NBA for *Jiji*, explained. "He is, as everybody says, definitely like MJ. There is nothing impossible for him. He is at the top of his game every season, and comes back at a higher level every year."

Like Mike, Ichiro has shown that he is unafraid of challenges. At the height of his career, having led his Bulls to three championships, Michael abruptly left the game to pursue a career in professional baseball. Ultimately he returned to basketball, but Mike had shown no fear in his willingness to try something new. Ichiro displayed a similar fearlessness in 2001 when he decided to leave his homeland to pursue his dream of playing American professional baseball.

Some Japanese pitchers had found success in the American game, which focuses on the strength and power of muscle-bound hitters. But no Japanese position player had ever made it in the American game. There were many observers who figured that the slightly built Ichiro would be quickly overpowered by America's high-speed pitchers, that he would not stack up as a hitter alongside larger teammates in the major leagues.

For others the news that Ichiro would attempt to play the American game was seen as merely the loss of another Japanese resource in a time when the country continued to be troubled by its seemingly always-stagnant economy. Amidst the headlines of bankruptcies and job layoffs now came the news that Ichiro was headed to America. It was as if there was a male identity crisis for all of Japan, *Time* magazine explained, adding that events served to "remind Japanese men so incessantly of their shortcomings that even alpha males are dizzy with self-doubt."

Perhaps that explains why all of Japan seemed to explode with pride when Ichiro stepped into a Seattle Mariners uniform in 2001 and produced an overwhelming display of finesse hitting and fierce fielding not seen since the days of, say, Shoeless Joe Jackson or Ty Cobb.

In America Ichiro was "merely" an instant, overwhelming success. Back home he was much more. He was a jolt of pride to a nation that sorely needed it.

That he had done it by taking such a huge risk was even more important. "Ichiro was doing really well in Japan. He was a big success," Yuichi Miketa, a 28-year-old government worker in Tokyo, told *Time*. "But he threw away everything and took a chance to go to America. That was quite a risk. But still he succeeded. It's a good lesson for Japan. I can't really take that kind of risk, but I wish I could."

Ichiro soon displayed his trademark concentration in America, stealing the hearts of baseball fans in Seattle. They saw that he was an immaculately disciplined ballplayer,

mentally sharp and wonderfully skilled in the fundamentals of the game.

From the apparent calm of his yoga warm-up routines, Ichiro would explode in each game with a show of heart that kept Seattle crowds roaring in delight. In the outfield he made running, diving catches. At the plate he hit and hit and hit and hit, turning back America's best pitchers with his unorthodox but highly effective style. On the bases he always seemed half a step ahead of his American counterparts. Off the field he was humble, but there was an air of supreme confidence behind those titanium shades.

Like Mike, there was a love for the game that seemed to leap right from his heart, and there was no question that his presence revitalized baseball just as Jordan's had rejuvenated basketball.

> Ichiro would explode in each game with a show of heart that kept Seattle crowds roaring in delight. Off the field he was humble, but with an air of confidence behind those titanium shades.

Best of all, perhaps, was Ichiro's determination to take responsibility for his actions. When Seattle lost a key game 1–0 to rival Anaheim in July 2002, manager Lou Piniella chose not to speak with reporters afterward. But Ichiro, who had made an uncharacteristic base-running error at a key moment, called the loss "the toughest one of my career" in Seattle.

It was obvious that each and every game mattered tremendously to Ichiro. He had come into the three-game series at Seattle's Safeco Field, part of a heated pennant race, leading the American League in batting. But his struggles at the plate against Anaheim meant that his team produced only 15 hits over the entire three games.

The toughest moment came in the eighth inning of the third game. Ichiro came to the plate of a scoreless game with one on and no one out. A buzz of anticipation coursed through the Safeco crowd.

Ichiro's bunts are often precise strikes to the heart of the defense, beautiful things to witness. But on this occasion his bunt was not placed well, and Anaheim third baseman Troy Glaus turned it into a force-out at second.

Still, Ichiro was on first and now had a chance to score the game's first run. When a wild pitch seemed to get away from Anaheim catcher Jose Molina, Ichiro made his break for second—the only problem being that he had misread the play. Molina hadn't let the ball get past him at all, and he quickly turned Ichiro's attempt into a trap and a rundown.

As Ichiro walked off the diamond in disappointment, the star's slumping shoulders showed how much he cared and how much he expected of himself. "Those are plays I must execute," he told reporters afterward. "I'm upset with myself when I don't execute plays that I'm supposed to make."

Like Mike, Ichiro has never hesitated to acknowledge his mistakes and to take responsibility for them. Like Mike, the necessity of those occasions is rare. He almost always seems to produce, and then produce some more.

Ichiro's usual offensive answer is a well-placed hit that finds a hole because he has studied the opponent's weaknesses. But he's also shown himself capable of outbursts of pure, American-style power.

In another July 2002 game he finished off the Texas Rangers with a three-run homer, the first three-run blast of his American career. It was obvious that Ichiro knew just what his team needed to keep pace in the pennant race with Anaheim.

"We knew before the game started that the Angels had won," he told reporters. "But does it make any difference? No. We always want to win."

The homer came with teammates Mike Cameron on third and Ben Davis on first and the game tied. Ichiro changed that with a shot to the right-field seats.

"The little fella hit a home run—who knows what that guy is going to do?" teammate Bret Boone said of Ichiro. "He gets hits every which way. Who knows how he does it?"

Home-run hitting is not Ichiro's focus, or his forte. His concern as Seattle's leadoff hitter is to get on base, something he has done with astounding regularity. Still, an outburst of six home runs during June and July of 2002 had reporters asking if he had begun to eye the fences.

"I'm not swinging for more power," Ichiro replied. "It's all about the angle of the bat through the pitches."

Just like it's about "being in the moment."

Like Mike, Ichiro has covered the angles and the moments with an inspiring display of heart and versatility. Like Mike, he honors the game. His performance has allowed him to assume a kind of stewardship of the game. We, in turn, hope to honor that effort with the text and photos on the ensuing pages.

For those who truly love baseball, it's obvious that the game is in good hands, which means that younger generations will be able to watch and see greatness and have the hope that they, too, can be "like Ichiro."

Chasing the Dream

Coming to America for Japanese baseball players has never been a simple thing. If nothing else, Masanori "Mashi" Murakami established that fact way back in 1964. The tug of war over his talents brought Major League Baseball into full conflict with Japanese baseball officials, and it would be years before conditions again allowed eastern talent to head west.

In 1964 the Nankai Hawks wanted three of their young players, including Murakami, to get more experience so they worked out a deal to send the trio to a San Francisco Giants' farm team. Of the three, Mashi Murakami made an immediate hit. The young pitcher would bow to his teammates whenever they turned a good play in support of his efforts on the mound, a show of respect that made him immediately popular in the dugout. It also didn't hurt that he did good things when he got the ball.

Gaining his teammates' trust as he moved along, Murakami posted 11 wins against 7 losses and managed to gain a promotion all the way to the "Show" itself when the Giants called him up that first season. San Francisco management eased him into the bigs with a road appearance at Shea Stadium against the cellar-dwelling Mets and about 50,000 of their best friends. He pitched one inning and didn't allow any runs.

From that unheralded beginning, Murakami went on to win one game and save another while posting a sleek 1.80 ERA. In all, he pitched 15 innings, during which he struck out 15 batters. Best of all, he walked just one. The Giants were so impressed that they made a grab for him, pointing out to the Hawks that his American contract actually allowed him to stay and play.

Stunned, the Japanese angrily argued that Murakami had only been loaned to the Giants under a gentlemen's agreement. Pretty soon, both sides claimed they had been insulted by the other. Then Major League Commissioner Ford Frick jumped into the fray, saying American baseball would sever its ties with the Japanese game if the Hawks didn't honor their contract.

Japanese baseball had long relied on American players to bolster the talent level in its leagues, and suddenly that supply of talent was threatened. Fortunately, before any more feelings were hurt, both sides came to their senses and worked out a deal. The Giants could have Murakami for one more season, after which he could choose where he wanted to play.

That second season proved a good one for Murakami. He won four with a single loss and saved another eight. He had a nifty 85 strikeouts in 74 innings. After the season's last game, he bowed politely to the Giants one last time and said he was heading for the home he badly missed.

It was 30 years before another Japanese pitcher ventured to follow in Mashi's footsteps.

Nomomania

Hideo Nomo was one of Japan's best pitchers in the early nineties, with a wicked hesitation windup that led to a variety of offspeed pitches and a touch of heat. But he grew dissatisfied with playing in his homeland. Quite simply, he considered himself good enough to play in America, and he wanted to prove that he could.

He wasted little time in doing just that after signing to play for the Los Angeles Dodgers in 1995. Once in L.A., he set about earning National League Rookie of the Year honors.

"I'm so glad I got to pitch in a real major league game," he told reporters after pitching his second game for the Dodgers. "This is what I always wanted. My dream was realized."

NOMOMANIA GRIPS L.A. AND JAPAN, the *L.A. Times* declared in a front-page story that July of 1995. Soon, though, Nomo's ride through American baseball would turn bumpy, and he would find himself making stops with several teams, all the while trying to prove that he belonged in the majors.

In the end Nomo would pay a high price for American stardom, which is one reason why journalist Akiko Yamawaki finds his story so compelling. "When he left Japan for the major leagues, which he had dreamed about for so long, everybody criticized him, saying, 'He thinks he can be successful in the major leagues, but he betrayed us, the Japanese

League,' " Yamawaki pointed out. "Ichiro would later get a little bit of criticism, but by the time he came to America, Japanese fans celebrated his new challenge even though they didn't want to see him leave. But Nomo had to go through a lot of hard times."

First the Dodgers traded him to the Mets, a team that ultimately released him in 1999. "When Nomo was released by the Mets in 1999, he had to try out for a new team," Yamawaki recalled. "The Cubs signed him to a minor league contract, but they released him too. He finally found a place to play in Milwaukee. In 2001 he opened the season with his second no-hitter, and now he is back with the Dodgers. Throughout all that, Nomo accepted the challenge alone and kept a positive mind. He is a very brave person. When you watch him pitch, you can sense how much of his heart he puts into baseball."

Nomo's countrymen followed him through these ups and downs, and their loyalty was rewarded on April 4, 2001, when Nomo, then pitching for the Red Sox, became the fourth pitcher in major league history to throw a no-hitter in both leagues, his second no-hitter resulting in a 3–0 victory over Baltimore.

Hideo Nomo

Certainly Nomo's results in America had been mixed, but the upside had been strong enough to convince the Yankees to go for another Japanese pitcher, Hideki Irabu, considered by some Japanese observers to be even better than Nomo.

The San Diego Padres owned Irabu's rights, but he made it clear that he would play in America only if he could play for the Yankees. This didn't exactly endear him to American baseball fans, but it pleased Yankee owner George Steinbrenner, who rewarded Irabu with a $12.8 million contract over four years, including an $8.5 million signing bonus. It was the most money ever given to a pitcher who had never made a major league appearance, and it sent a signal to Japan's best players that America offered them a genuine opportunity for wealth and fame.

There were others, of course, who had already begun to discover that, including Mac Suzuki, notable as the third Japanese-born player in the major leagues. He was actually the first in the American League when he debuted with the Mariners in 1996. He was also unique in that he never played professionally in Japan before joining the Mariners. He appeared in about two dozen games in Seattle before moving on to Kansas City in 1999 and to the Colorado Rockies in 2001.

Another Japanese player to find success in the majors was Kazuhiro Sasaki, whose nickname is "Daimajin," or "Big Demon." An accomplished reliever who had spent a decade as the property of the Yokohama Bay Stars (also known as the Yokohama Taiyo Whales), Sasaki signed with Seattle in late 1999 and was named the AL Rookie of the Year in 2000 after registering 37 saves for the Mariners (third in the league).

The success of this run of Japanese pitchers prompted two position players to finally act on their own dreams as 2000 came to a close. They were Ichiro Suzuki, the Pacific League's batting champion for seven consecutive seasons, and Tsuyoshi Shinjo, a slugger for the Hanshin Tigers.

The announcement by Ichiro came as no great surprise in Japan, where reports had surfaced over the years that he dreamed of playing in the United States. There was even speculation that he could draw offers exceeding $10 million. In fact, the Mariners would wind up paying over $13 million to bring Ichiro to their roster for the 2001 season.

To prove that he was ready, Ichiro had spent his last season in Japan hitting .387, breaking his own record for the best batting average in Japanese history. In the process he won a seventh straight batting title and improved his lifetime average to .353. Across Japan, baseball fans knew they were losing a legend.

The Story Unfolds

Ichiro was born on October 22, 1973, in Kasugai, which is part of the Aichi prefecture. By age three he was already demonstrating his skill with a bat and ball. By age eight he was telling anyone who would listen that baseball was his love.

He wanted to play on a team, so finally his father relented and allowed Ichiro to join the town team. To make sure that things went well, the elder Suzuki signed on as the team's manager.

The team practiced only on Sundays, but one advantage of living with the manager is that you can coax him into some one-on-one workouts, which is what Ichiro did, badgering his old man to come out and work with him every day. This went on for about four years until Ichiro was old enough to go to high school.

At first the coaches there weren't convinced of his abilities, but Ichiro's determination eventually won them over. Once it did, his high school team made a quick rise—Ichiro gave his whole heart and mind to baseball. "He told one American writer that he studied hard in junior high and got good scores," Yamawaki recalled. "But his scores started falling in high school, where his number-one priority was baseball and practicing hard."

His superior play twice propelled his high school team into the "Koshien," which is Japan's national high school baseball tournament. "The high school baseball tournament is very big in Japan," Yamawaki explained, "like the 'March Madness' of American college basketball. In August many Japanese baseball fans go crazy about the high school baseball tournament."

By the time he finished high school in 1991, Ichiro was so well developed that the Orix Blue Waves selected him in the fourth round of the draft. He was immediately assigned to the Blue Waves' minor league affiliate in 1992, where he hit .366 in 58 games.

It didn't take the Blue Waves' management too long to do the math. Ichiro was on his way to becoming a great hitter, and his fielding was superb. He was called up to the majors that first season but batted only .253 in 40 games.

The next year Ichiro again played for both the farm and major league teams. He again tore up the minors, hitting .371 with 8 home runs in 48 games. In the majors, however, his numbers plummeted to .188 with 1 home run in 64 at-bats.

Regardless, Ichiro was on his way. He hit his first professional homer on June 12, 1993, against the Kinetsu Buffaloes. The opposing pitcher? Hideo Nomo.

Then, all of a sudden, he broke away from the pack in 1994, hitting .385 and setting a Japanese baseball record with 210 hits in just 130 games. From May 21 through August 26 of that year he got on base in 69 straight games, another record. The entire performance made him the overwhelming choice as the Pacific League MVP.

With his success in 1994, Ichiro discovered the downside of athletic greatness: the intense pressure to keep performing at a high level. "He has been under pressure since 1994, when he set those Japanese baseball records with 210 hits in 130 games and won his first batting title with a .385 average," Yamawaki observed. "Since that year, Ichiro's name has been everywhere in Japan. Everybody expects to see his best every game, every single move. And he has responded with winning the batting title six more seasons, along with many other records. However, he has felt pressure. I think mostly from himself."

In December 1995 Ichiro made one of his journeys to America and was able to visit with Michael Jordan on the set of a TV show. "At that time he asked Jordan how he handled the pressure," Yamawaki recalled. "And Jordan told him not to make it difficult, just have fun with baseball, and that the same is true in life."

Jordan later told Yoko Miyaji, another noted Japanese journalist, "Ichiro was concerned about the expectations hanging over him, so I told him that it's impossible to play to the media and the fans' expectations. So just have fun with the pressure and enjoy baseball."

That would prove to be most valuable advice, but it would still take time for Ichiro to learn to deal with the pressure. He continued to struggle with the issue, even as he continued to dominate Japanese baseball. "Everyone said my batting had been great, but I felt I was in the abyss," Ichiro would later recall, saying that he told himself to keep working hard, developing his skill at the plate, using his determination to mold himself into the ultimate batsman.

As Jordan himself did, Ichiro came to see the pressure as a positive. "He said he could find his way because he felt fans' expectations and his responsibility to the team," Yamawaki explained.

"If it was about mentality or depression, I can handle my self-control," Ichiro later revealed in a book. "But it was about my skill of offense, so it wasn't easy."

Yamawaki noted, "There is a phrase he often uses: 'This is about baseball, what I really love.'

"This is basic for him," the Japanese reporter explained. "He dreams, trains hard, challenges, never gives up, and reaches to the next level because he loves it."

Those things worked famously for Ichiro over the ensuing seasons. He led the Pacific League with a career-high 49 stolen bases in 1995, good enough to earn league MVP honors for a second straight year. Best of all, he set a career-high with 25 home runs. He followed that with yet another MVP award in 1996, and another batting crown. Powered by this outburst, the Blue Waves won the pennant that year and went on to defeat the Yomiuri Giants in the championship series.

All of these things prompted manager Akira Ogi to make that name change on Ichiro's jersey in 1997. Ichiro rewarded the gesture by making a Japanese-record 216 straight plate appearances without striking out from April 16 to June 25. The season also brought another batting title and another pennant for the Blue Waves.

At that point, Ichiro's life seemed like nothing but a series of milestones whizzing past in his rearview mirror. He registered his 1,000th hit on April 20, 1999, against Nippon in the Tokyo Dome. About three months later, in early July, he connected on his 100th home run, against the Seibu Lions.

Suddenly trouble appeared on the landscape. A wayward pitch broke the ulna bone in his right hand in August of 1999. Although he managed to finish with a sixth straight batting title, (.343), his 2000 season fell prey to a strained right rib-cage muscle in late August. Nevertheless, Ichiro continued his string of batting titles, All-Star appearances, Gold Glove Awards, and other honors.

Amidst all that success, he continued to wonder if there could be more to life. Like his idol, Jordan, Ichiro was unafraid of finding out the answer to that very intriguing question.

2001: An Ichiro Odyssey

Natsuki Une is the editor of *Slugger*, the monthly Japanese magazine that covers professional baseball. Une first heard of Ichiro Suzuki as a bright young pitcher and outfielder playing in Japan's national high school baseball tournament.

Une recalls watching Ichiro play and coming away unimpressed. "When he was a high school player, he was very thin," Une said in an August 2002 interview. "So I didn't think he would be special, and of course not a major leaguer."

Une is obviously far too principled to jump on the Ichiro bandwagon. The Japanese editor acknowledges Ichiro's effectiveness, but he doesn't pretend that he saw it coming.

Of course Une was far from alone in that perspective. Even Ichiro's first professional coach had trouble seeing his potential and didn't place him in the starting lineup.

Word on the street in Japan was that Ichiro and his father, Nobuyuki "Chichiro" Suzuki, had perfected his unorthodox batting style a few yen at a time by feeding the coin-operated batting machines at a local batting center. The implication, perhaps, was that the young player had a "nickel-and-dime" kind of game.

A few years later Une recalled watching Ichiro on his way to the 1994 Pacific League batting title. This time the editor was impressed with Ichiro's speed. But Une seems cautious about getting caught up in the Ichiro worship that enraptures many Japanese fans.

"Everybody in Japan knows his name," Une offered. "But as an MLB player, Hideo Nomo's impact is bigger than Ichiro's. Many Japanese think MLB is about power. Nomo got many strikeouts from MLB's power hitters. Ichiro cannot get many home runs from MLB's power pitchers. He can get a hit."

He can get a hit? That, in a nutshell, sums up the perspective of those who are reserved in their praise of Ichiro. American baseball is all about power, has been since the Babe Ruth revolution turned the game on its ear with his thundering home runs in the twenties.

Ichiro, on the other hand, is not about power, at least not the conventional power that both the fans and media have come to expect from modern, steroid-enhanced baseball.

Against the Odds

There were few who predicted Ichiro would be an overwhelming success when he joined the Seattle Mariners for the 2001 season. For Ichiro, coming to America meant having an opportunity to refute the naysayers. It meant he could show that his speed in itself was a new kind of power, one that would ultimately make his American opponents very uneasy.

To their credit, the Mariners obviously believed in him. They paid $13.125 million to bring him in as the first position player from Japan in the American big leagues.

If any team was prepared to risk such money on Ichiro, it was the Mariners. His addition meant that of all the teams in the majors, they had the most Japanese-born players—three, including pitchers Kazuhiro Sasaki and Shigetoshi Hasegawa.

The Mariners also desperately needed a productive player, having lost the fabulous Alex Rodriguez, the famed "A-Rod," to a whopping free-agency offer in excess of $200 million from the Texas Rangers. The loss of Rodriguez had deeply embittered many loyal Mariners fans, and the team knew it needed to make a few moves to remain competitive.

The situation, of course, only served to heap more pressure on Ichiro. Not only was he carrying the hopes of millions of Japanese, but he would also be making every move under the watchful eye of millions of Mariners fans in the Pacific Northwest.

Well before the 2001 season, however, Ichiro had taken Michael Jordan's advice about dealing with pressure to heart. The now 28-year-old Japanese star was possessed of a supreme confidence—not a loud, raucous attitude, but a quiet, low-key forbearance. His determination emanated from behind his titanium shades and manifested itself in every brilliant detail of his game, from his immaculate mental preparation right down to his careful cleaning of his spikes and his studious adjusting of equipment. He sought to maximize every facet of his approach so that nothing would stand in the way of him doing his best.

"He was so cool," says Akiko Yamawaki, sportswriter for *Jiji Press*. "Everything he dreamed would come true."

If only millions of his countrymen could have known that in advance, it might have saved them much anxiety. It seemed that news about Ichiro was everywhere you turned in Japan. There was even a new film coming out, titled *Run, Ichiro*.

The live broadcast of Ichiro's first game with the Mariners aired on a satellite channel at 11:00 A.M. Tokyo time, when many fans were at school or working. Others were intensely following the live national coverage of the extremely popular high school baseball tournament on another channel.

Among the hundreds of thousands able to see Ichiro's first Mariners game on TV, the nervous anxiety rose when he grounded out in his first two at-bats in the major leagues. Things did not look good. Then came his third trip to the plate. He struck out.

Suddenly the worst fears of many Japanese fans seemed to be coming true. Ichiro would embarrass himself and dishonor his sport and his country. It would be a global display of ineptitude that a dozen Hideo Nomos couldn't repair. Once again, the Japanese would be the laughingstock of the sporting world.

Ichiro Suzuki, the dominator of Japanese baseball, was about to bomb in the American game.

There were many who groaned, turned off the TV set, and walked away that day, unable to witness the debacle. What they missed was seeing Ichiro single in his next two at-bats to finish the day at two for five—a .400 hitter in his first day.

News of Ichiro's success swelled Japan with pride that evening. Yet it still couldn't help the Orix Blue Waves at the gate that night. Just a season before, with No. 51, Ichiro, in the lineup, the Waves had averaged 18,000 fans a night. On the evening of his first American game, they drew only 800.

In the crowd was fan Masato Fujii, who had sat in right field encouraging Ichiro on defense through many nights. "I miss him so much," Fujii told American reporter Jim Caple.

"It's a little complicated to explain to a little kid why Ichiro went to the United States," another fan said. "But that's what he chose to do. He's doing the same thing as [Mariners reliever] Kazuhiro Sasaki. The American players come over here and the Japanese players go over there, and that's the way it is."

"I think he will hit .350," another fan, Hiso Kirai, said. "He has the heritage of Japan with him, he will do very well. Not just with his hitting, but with his arm, his fielding, his running, everything.

"Ichiro is still the property of Japan, so I like him. And I want him to prove that Japanese players can play in America as well."

Even after his big opening day, there were many doubters who figured Ichiro would wilt when facing all that heat from American pitchers. Instead he gave them a little heat of his own to worry about. After one week as the Mariners' leadoff hitter, he was batting .417.

Eyebrows were raised on at least two continents. They grew wider when, at the end of the first month of the season, he was leading the league in batting.

Suddenly, large numbers of Japanese Americans started showing up at ballparks around the league, eager to learn more about Ichiro. Many of them drove long distances to see him.

Yuka Yonashiro, a 23-year-old, said she drove three hours in hopes of seeing Ichiro smile. "I just want to watch him," Yonashiro told a reporter as she watched Ichiro take batting practice one day. "I expect that he'll have a hit, make a steal.

"He never shows his smile," she said.

"When he went to the United States, everyone was very disappointed," said Yasufuki Suzuki, another Japanese American. "But I am happy to see him here."

"Of everything he did in his first year, it's hard to believe that he adjusted to the major leagues so quickly and became a top-level player," journalist Yamawaki said, looking

back during an August 2002 interview. "When he was in Japan, Jason Giambi, Ken Griffey Jr., Barry Bonds . . . those players were his idols, and he reached the same level as them immediately.

"He was excited to play against Sosa, Bonds, and Curt Schilling. Especially when he played against Schilling, he couldn't hide his coolness. Schilling was a new type of pitcher and a challenge to him.

"You could see how much he enjoyed the challenge. This part of him reminds me of Kobe Bryant," added Yamawaki, who also covers the Los Angeles Lakers on a regular basis.

Better yet, the Mariners, ignited by Ichiro's overall play, rolled out a huge lead in the American League West and never looked back in the pennant race.

Coping with Success

Ichiro, meanwhile, had become very big news in Japan. A horde of Japanese reporters followed his every move. They especially wanted to know how badly he coveted an American League batting crown. After all, he had won seven straight titles in Japan.

"Everything he did was a big story in Japan," said Yamawaki, who reported on his games for *Jiji*. "Since the middle of June when he first led the league in batting average, our questions were often about it. But every time his answer was the same: 'I don't play for batting average. I play for wins.'"

He also wanted to be named Rookie of the Year, an honor that had already been accorded two of his countrymen in previous seasons, Yamawaki said. "Unlike MVP, he said that 'I will get Rookie of the Year naturally if I play my baseball.'"

Unfortunately, the Japanese media wanted to report about much more than Ichiro's baseball feats. The tabloids, in particular, were amazingly aggressive in seeking details about his private life. There were reports that he knew a Japanese gangster, that he had had an affair with a married woman, that he had another relationship with a woman in San Francisco.

"If they could, they would want breaking news about Ichiro all the time," Yamawaki said of the aggressive tabloids and TV stations. "For example, 'Ichiro is involved with the Yakuza [the Japanese mafia]; Ichiro had an affair with a married woman; 'Ichiro slept with a woman in San Francisco. . . .' He is sick of it, so he doesn't want any media taking advantage of him."

Ichiro even decided to get married in Los Angeles rather than face the paparazzi in Japan. "In Japan, the media invaded my privacy so much," Ichiro explained to a Mariners' media representative. "They would even watch me go to the haircut place or a restaurant. Then they would interview the people at the haircutters."

The last straw was a rumor that a Japanese magazine had offered $2 million for a nude photo of Ichiro. "I would do it," he told the Mariners' media rep, "if the people who take the photo, if the people who yank my leg and invade my privacy, if they would disappear."

"You mean you would do it if they would stop writing about you and following you?" the Mariners interviewer asked.

"No," Ichiro replied. "If they would disappear from the planet."

Finally, both Ichiro Suzuki and teammate Sasaki decided they'd had enough of the Japanese media covering their lives. The two players issued a joint statement saying they would not talk to the Japanese press corps until further notice.

"Their position is that it's important their privacy away from the ballpark be respected," said Tim Hevly, director of media relations for the Mariners. "And until such time that they feel the Japanese media gives them that respect, they will be unable to speak with Japanese media."

"There are rules to cover Ichiro," Yamawaki explained. "It's a little bit different because we cannot talk to Ichiro directly. [We] don't interview him individually. [We can't] be there when Ichiro talks to American media. There is only one reporter who represents all Japanese media for interviews. Other reporters can get his comments through the person later so there is no original comment for any Japanese media. There is a Mariners PR person around him after the game, and when any Japanese media get close to him, they are stopped."

The ban left more than 30 Japanese reporters standing by each game, silently watching Ichiro go through his pregame routines. They would watch the game, then stand back afterward, unable to interview him.

To get around the ban Japanese reporters began getting their info from American beat writers "because Ichiro will talk to American media more than Japanese media," Yamawaki explained. "I don't know why he is so tough on Japanese media. But on the other hand, I think he doesn't want any media trying to take advantage of him."

To speak to his Japanese fans Ichiro "released two books last year, one during the 2001 season and another after the season. These books are based on Ichiro's interviews about many things including family, life, and his dreams," Yamawaki said. "I don't know if this is good for Ichiro or not, but it has become his way of dealing with media. There are writers who have covered Ichiro since he played in Japan and who know each other. Ichiro talks personally to some media he really can believe in. Those people won't write any breaking news about his personal life.

"Other media can say hello to him but they don't talk to him. There might be some normal conversation, but it's unlikely because he feels betrayed by media. He will not talk to any new media that he does not trust," Yamawaki explained.

"I want him to open up to media more," she said, "but on the other hand, it's understandable. He is so big in Japan. If you become popular in Japan, this kind of thing is top news all the time. That's why there are a lot of gossip magazines and newspapers in Japan. Any story about Ichiro, you can imagine how much [the publication's] sales go up. Famous people like Ichiro become a big target. He admitted he slept with a married woman. When the news was released he had already been married and had already signed with the Mariners. I guess he admitted the relationship and doesn't talk about it anymore so he [can] focus on his new challenge."

Part of the intense media interest in Ichiro is driven in Japan by people other than sports fans, Yamawaki added. "He is attractive to women. Even though he is married, still a lot of women love him. Not only is he a great baseball player, he is good looking, slim, and clever. So many women are crazy about him. Yes, he has had several scandals with women, but he has never showed immaturity. He is kind of quiet and serious about what he is doing."

Ichiro wasn't exactly in love with American reporters, either, during his first season in Seattle. He spoke to them through an interpreter and seemed mostly amused by their questions.

Asked what he liked about America, Ichiro didn't hesitate. "I like the fans," he said. "I like the attitude they take to baseball. Their passion as fans is very high."

Laughing Matters

The American fans, in turn, have shown a great appreciation for their surprising new hero. "They have fallen in love with Ichiro," Yamawaki said. "I was at Safeco Field when Alex Rodriguez first came back as a Ranger. Seattle fans loved him, but they were also left heartbroken by him. All the fans that day in sold-out Safeco Field united like those noisy Sacramento Kings fans in the NBA. They booed Rodriguez so loud. It was April, still early in the season. Seattle fans are happy now after what the Mariners did in 2001. And they have found a new hero in Ichiro instead of A-Rod."

Some Mariners fans have been moved to poetry by the sight of Ichiro: "He came from the land of the rising sun," goes one fan song.

"He's No. 51.

"Can't believe how fast that guy can run.

"Go, go Ichiro.

"You're my, my hero."

Fans also expressed that love in the 2001 All-Star vote. At the All-Star break Ichiro led the major leagues with 126 hits and 27 stolen bases. He had the American League's second-best batting average at .349. But he topped everyone with 3,373,035 All-Star votes, which made him the first rookie starter since Nomo in 1995.

The vote was huge news in Japan, Yamawaki recalled. "I cannot remember how many articles I wrote that day. He had the day off and didn't play as a starter [in] the game after the announcement. All of a sudden, he came out as a pinch-hitter during the seventh inning, but he struck out. Then he hit a two-run, game-tying home run in the top of the ninth inning, and the Mariners won the game. It was so emotional that day."

Narumi Komatsu, who has written a book on Ichiro, told an American interviewer how he felt when Ichiro was announced as an All-Star starter. "As fans chanted, 'I-CHI-RO, I-CHI-RO,' I felt very proud," Komatsu said.

"Imagine. Americans cheering for a Japanese player in their national pastime."

Before Ichiro, Komatsu said, "Japan was associated with products. Objects. Sony stuff. This is the first time Japan has been [known for] its men."

A serious, hard-working journalist, Yamawaki said she was very surprised at how quickly Ichiro captured hearts in America. "I thought he would be successful, but not [this much]. He went to the top so quickly. I think Ichiro was surprised too. Because when he led All-Star votes and was selected as a starter, he said he had already gotten tickets for the All-Star Game. It was held in his home stadium, Safeco Field, so he was looking forward to seeing it as a fan."

The All-Star Game served to push interest in Ichiro to a new level, Yamawaki said. "After that, wherever the Mariners traveled, everyone was so excited to see this new Japanese player. They talked about him on the front pages of every town's sports section. The local sports reporters grabbed Japanese reporters and asked a lot of questions about him. I was asked by the American media several times, 'Is it true that there are many Japanese who can tell you Ichiro's name but cannot remember the emperor's name?' I told them I thought it was true. He is one of the most important people in Japan, and everyone is proud of him."

With his bat, his speed on the bases, his glove, and his arm, Ichiro led the Mariners to an amazing 116 victories in 2001, tying a 95-year-old mark for most wins in a season. He won the American League batting title at .350, Rookie of the Year honors, *and* the Most Valuable Player award—an incredible feat. He was the first player since Fred Lynn in 1975 to receive both the MVP Award and Rookie of the Year honors.

Ichiro paced the majors in hits (242). Among his many broken records was most hits by a rookie, which was set by the legendary Shoeless Joe Jackson in 1911. Ichiro also led the league in steals.

"As a hitter," Yamawaki said admiringly, "he did whatever was needed to get on base: bunt, run so fast, slide. Even when it was difficult for him to get a hit from a pitcher, he would find a way. He would hit a ground ball to an infielder where he could take advantage of his speed and get an infield hit.

"As a right fielder, he has great vision and can move so quickly. He never gives up, and he has a strong arm. During games—on the bench, in right field, in the on-deck circle—you can see him always stretching. Maybe because of the style of Japanese baseball where every little thing, like sacrifice plays, are very valuable things to do, that's why little things mean so much to him for the team."

The strain of doing all of those things for so many people in Japan and America was obvious, Yamawaki said. "During the season, sometimes I could see his joy and pleasure, but it was muted with the strain of the season. When he got the MVP last fall, it was the first time I heard the real sound of his laugh.

"He was so relaxed, accepting the honor of the MVP. And he finally laughed."

High-Speed Thrills

Ichiro throws right but he bats left, which, of course, puts him a few critical steps closer to first base. After slapping the ball into the infield, it takes him just 3.7 seconds to reach first.

This puts incredible pressure on opposing defenses. As soon as Ichiro slap-hits the ball into the infield, even the best shortstops have reason to pause and worry, all the while thinking, "3.7 seconds . . ."

He's about to show them up, to reveal that they're a tick slow in getting to the ball, scooping it up, and getting the throw off.

If anything revealed this Ichiro phenomenon, it was the first round of the 2001 American League playoffs. Ichiro and his Mariner teammates faced the Cleveland Indians, who featured perhaps the best defensive infield duo in the business: Omar Vizquel and Roberto Alomar.

Ichiro set them on edge with every ground ball. On the day that the Mariners clinched their comeback victory over the Indians, Ichiro had three infield singles in Seattle's 3–1 win.

Vizquel would field a well-hit grounder only to have Ichiro beat his throw. "How can I make a better play than that?" Vizquel asked reporters afterward. "That was the only chance I had on a ball to my left. I tried to get rid of the ball as quick as possible. But the guy just flies. If he hits a ground ball two steps to your left or to your right, it's going to be a tough out. You have to field the ball clean, and then make a perfect throw.

"If he hits the ball anywhere near the hole, it's a sure base hit."

"That's the kind of pressure he puts on a defense," said Mariners center fielder Mike

Cameron. "And we just played the best defense, as far as middle infielders go—Vizquel and Robbie Alomar. He hits the ball on the ground. And he doesn't just put the ball in play. He hits it hard on the ground, and he's got two steps on the defense already. They say you can't outrun a baseball, but he's shown me many a time this year that he can probably do it."

The Indians had taken a 2–1 lead in the series. For Game 4 they sent out their ace, Bartolo Colon. But they couldn't overcome Ichiro's speed.

For the five-game series he hit .600 on 12 hits in 20 at-bats, a new record for a five-game AL division series. More important, he scored a quarter of the Mariners' 16 runs in the series. Ichiro's 12 hits also tied an ALDS record, set in 1995 by Edgar Martinez.

"Ichiro is a heck of a leadoff hitter," Charlie Manuel, then the Indians manager, told reporters. "I don't know how we stop him."

"I don't know whether I had a good swing or not," Ichiro said afterward. "The only thing I could tell is that I fared well in this series."

"What he did in the postseason, that shouldn't happen. It's unfair," Indians general manager John Hart said.

High Praise

The New York Yankees, awaiting the Mariners in the American League Championship Series, had similar thoughts. "It's tough," Yankees pitcher Andy Pettitte, slated to start Game 1, said of facing Ichiro. "He causes chaos when he gets on. You've got to worry about him because you realize he can steal. You've got to bring the infielders in a little bit because you realize that he's swinging as he runs out of the box and can just beat out a ground ball to any of the infielders.

"Obviously he's a big part of the reason they have had the season they've had."

The Mariners were delighted with their "purchase" of Ichiro—they had plunked down nearly $14 million just for the right to sign him and will pay him $15 million over three years.

"We knew we were getting a good player when we signed him, a good athlete and a good player," Mariners manager Lou Piniella said. "Now, did we think he was going to get 244 hits? Did we think he was going to get [12] hits in the first round of the playoffs? Lead the league in hitting? I don't think anybody is that smart."

Despite his small size, Ichiro clearly stood up to the rigors of the lengthy American baseball season, with more in his tank for the playoffs.

"He weighs about a buck-40 and he hasn't worn down and hasn't gotten hurt," Seattle reliever Norm Charlton said. "He's still playing like it's April."

Somehow, through all the challenges, he even maintained a sense of humor, which he apparently used to mask his anxiety over the challenge.

"I think he's a clown," Charlton said.

"It's comedy," Bret Boone agreed. "It really is comedy, the way he's getting on base. It's unbelievable."

"Every day I'm nervous," Ichiro said. "Not one day goes by when I'm not nervous."

"He makes a mockery of hitting itself," Cameron said. "The guy is unbelievable when it comes to putting the bat on the ball."

"What doesn't he do?" Charlton said. "He's got all the tools. He runs, he hits, he throws. Really, the only thing he doesn't do is hit 50 home runs. And if he wanted to do that, he probably could."

"You really can't point a finger at any part of his game that he doesn't excel at," Cameron said. "Mentally, he's like the Statue of Liberty. He never gets fazed by anything."

"He works at his craft," Mariners pitcher Jamie Moyer said. "And to me, that's what makes him the player he is."

The Big Stage

Yet all the accolades quieted very quickly in the league championship series, when the Mariners as a team discovered just why the Yankees are a dynasty. To a man, Seattle struggled and promptly lost both games at Safeco.

Now Ichiro and his teammates faced the arduous task of going into Yankee Stadium and winning during the playoffs in Games 3, 4, and 5. "It's not an easy place to play," ex-Yankee Piniella said. "If you don't have confidence, it can intimidate you, there's no question about it. The crowd is loud, raucous, and there are a lot of bars around the ballpark, so the fans come in there prepared."

The Mariners' confidence was based on their 59 road wins during the regular season, including five in New York. "In general, we've played pretty well in New York since I have been here," Piniella said. "When you have a better ballclub like we have, we can handle the situation well."

The series had a pall cast over it, since it was played in New York just a matter of weeks after the September 11 terrorist attacks. "I don't really look that much forward to going there," Piniella said. "But we are going to do everything we can as an organization, as a team. If they need us to do some things to help out in any way, we're certainly going to be available for that. But as far as getting close to Ground Zero, no, I wouldn't want to do that."

New York manager Joe Torre had already shown a keen ability to adjust to the new offensive threat that Ichiro posed. With a one-run lead in Game 2, Torre intentionally walked Ichiro in the top of the seventh. For the Yankee boss the move was not unorthodox. Ichiro was hitting .468 with runners in scoring position and two outs. Next up came Mark McLemore, who grounded to first.

"There's not many rookies you're going to walk, but he's a special player," Torre said. "No disrespect to McLemore, but Ichiro just puts the ball in play too much and gets too many hits."

In Game 3 the move backfired. Torre again walked Ichiro, loading the bases, and McLemore responded, helping to boost the Mariners to a 14–3 win that cut the Yankee series lead to 2–1.

They would get no closer, however. The Yankee defense would tighten for a Game 4 win. Entering Game 5, Ichiro was hitting .231 in the series. The Yankees were coming at him with a new pitching strategy.

"I don't think it is any one place," Torre told the writers. "You really have to move the [strike] zone around on him because he's too good of a hitter and he is going to make adjustments.

"I think we have had success getting him out because we have changed [the pitching pattern] not only at-bat to at-bat, but pitch to pitch. The only thing we knew going in is that he was too good of a hitter to pitch the same way all the time."

In Game 5 Piniella switched right fielder Ichiro with left fielder Jay Buhner. Because Yankee Stadium's left field is so vast, Piniella needed Ichiro's speed to cover the territory. It was his first American appearance in left field.

Ultimately, though, it was too late. The Mariners could not stop the Yankee machine. Ichiro was bitterly disappointed and took more than his share of the blame for a team failure.

Fundamental in his approach, though, was his fearlessness in competition. Even though the season was over, he was eager to get back at it.

Restless Heart

Ichiro Suzuki won virtually every major award in the big leagues during his first season, 2001. He broke several of the game's age-old records, replacing legendary names such as Jackie Robinson and Shoeless Joe Jackson. He sparked his team to an incredible 116 wins.

But winning was what truly mattered, and Ichiro was truly hurt after the 2001 playoffs.

During the off-season he toured the Baseball Hall of Fame in Cooperstown, New York, with his wife, Yumiko, to see baseball's American treasures.

Although he still spoke mostly through an interpreter, Ichiro began to gain more confidence with his English. In fact, one of his often-repeated messages to fans was, "I'm looking forward to seeing you at Safeco Field." His presence was one of several reasons that Seattle's ballpark had an attendance of 3.5 million people in 2001.

They would come in droves again for 2002, a factor presaged by the throngs at the Mariners spring-training site in Arizona. One writer watched a crowd intently following some activity at spring training and asked, "What's going on over there?"

"Ichiro is tying his shoes," someone replied.

He held court for the media on a stool in front of his spring-training locker and was quickly asked about his goals for 2002. Ichiro didn't want to reveal them. "Of course I had expectations of myself, and of course I have them again this year," he replied. "Both of them were extremely high levels of expectations.

"The goals that I set are for me to perform the best that I possibly can," he added. "More than getting better every day or improving every day, it's more being able to show your best performance every day. That's what I strive for."

Some reporters wondered if the upcoming season wouldn't be easier, now that he was adjusted to the American game and knew what to expect from all those heat-throwing pitchers. "I have more information than last year. They have more information too," Ichiro said.

"Obviously, I'm more comfortable than last year, but there will still be some difficult things that I have to overcome," he said. "It's never the same pitcher, the same style, so I will just be prepared for every at-bat, whatever I get."

Unlimited Potential

At 5'9" and 160 pounds in his rookie year, Ichiro was a finely tuned hitting and running machine, the first player to lead the majors in both batting average and stolen bases since Jackie Robinson accomplished that feat in 1949.

With so many strengths, it was only natural that observers would scan his stats for areas of improvement. He hit only eight home runs in 2001, which created an active area of inquiry headed into the 2002 season: would he display more power?

"To ask him, as an MVP, to be better is asking a lot," said Mets manager Bobby Valentine, who managed against Ichiro in Japan in 1995. "But he will be better. He'll hit home runs, and a lot of them."

"I had a couple of Japanese writers tell me that he would hit 30 home runs this year," Mariners manager Lou Piniella told reporters. "I think if he hits eight to twelve home runs, that's plenty. That's not what we got him here for."

Yet Piniella has privately acknowledged to Valentine that if the Mariners were to hold an intrasquad home-run derby, Ichiro would come out on top, evidenced by his daily performances in batting practice. He literally put the ball anywhere he wanted: deep, short, left, right, middle, over the fence—it didn't matter.

If Ichiro regularly produced home runs, they would be shots pulled to the right, a product of his combination of a packed swing, bat control, great hands, and balance. "He can hit 30 home runs in a blink and a half," the Mets' Valentine insisted.

"Ichiro is the best Japanese import to come along since the VCR," wrote one scribe in assessing his approach.

Ichiro had rushed out of the gate in 2001, getting at least one hit in 40 of his first 43 games with the Mariners. He had run off a 15-game hitting streak from April 4 to April 20 and then hit in 23 straight games from April 22 to May 18.

In 2002 he opened decidedly slower, hitting just .250 with no homers and just one extra-base hit in his first six games. No one, especially his teammates, blinked. They knew he would get it going.

"He's pretty good, huh?" Mark McLemore said. "I guess he's got it figured out now. Last year he hit .350 blind. No telling what he'll do now that he's figured it out."

Sure enough, his average soon soared to .384 after a .476 clip through a 15-game hit streak. Suddenly Ichiro was fielding questions about the possibility of the almost mythical .400, the range last reached by Ted Williams, who hit .406 in 1941. Ichiro moved quickly to silence that talk.

"No. Never. A number is not my goal," he said.

Whatever It Takes

Whatever the average, his hitting was critical to the Mariners, who seemed stalled trying to follow up on their 116 wins in 2001.

"Ichiro is about as hot as he can be, but we need more from a lot of the guys," Piniella told reporters. The manager even moved Ichiro from leadoff to the number three spot in the lineup on one road trip, trying to rev up production in a Mariners offense struggling with Mike Cameron, Bret Boone, and Jeff Cirillo all hitting under .250.

Through one 39-game stretch of the summer of 2002, the Mariners went 20–19, staying just a game or two ahead of surprisingly pesky Anaheim.

"We have some mistakes in games. We can adjust," Ichiro said through an interpreter. His humble approach and positive nature helped keep the clubhouse atmosphere light.

"I'm jealous," Boone joked. "I ask him how come I can't get hits like that? How come I can't bounce one off the plate? But Ichiro shouldn't count. He plays a different game. He puts the ball in play. He doesn't have to be swinging good. He's halfway to first base and if he slaps the ball in the hole, he can get a hit any time he wants to get a hit.

"Ichiro's different. He doesn't try to do anything else. He knows what his job is, and he doesn't try to overdo it. To his credit, that's what makes him a great player. He takes his game and doesn't get greedy."

Yet Ichiro, like any great player, has had his troubles, too. As July turned to August, the Mariners put together a five-game winning streak to move their record to 68–42, a season-high 26 games over .500.

Ichiro, meanwhile, went 5-for-33 in one eight-game streak and saw his batting average fall from .363 to .347.

Still, his teammates didn't worry. The mood had lifted, and they knew that Ichiro would soon be right back on top of the ball. "The last week it's been better," Piniella said of his team's offense. "We struggled there for a while."

To help their resurgence, a record 46,219 fans came out to create the largest Safeco Field gathering in regular-season history. What they saw was what they came for: Ichiro laying it all on the line every single game, hitting, running, stealing, throwing, defending, all of it just shy of the speed of sound.

"The reason why many of his teammates love him is that he does everything to win," said reporter Akiko Yamawaki. "He is always ready, defensively, offensively, and mentally."

All the while his opponents, like the fans, are busy thinking, "What's he gonna do next?" The answer is simple: very big things.